super simple
twig projects

FUN AND EASY CRAFTS INSPIRED BY NATURE

Kelly Doudna

Consulting Editor, Diane Craig, M.A./Reading Specialist

A Division of ABDO

ABDO
Publishing Company

visit us at www.abdopublishing.com

Published by ABDO Publishing Company, a division of ABDO, P.O. Box 398166, Minneapolis, Minnesota 55439.

Printed in the United States of America, North Mankato, Minnesota
102013
012014

 PRINTED ON RECYCLED PAPER

Editor: Liz Salzmann
Content Developer: Nancy Tuminelly
Cover and Interior Design and Production: Kelly Doudna, Mighty Media, Inc.
Photo Credits: Kelly Doudna, Shutterstock

The following manufacturer's name appearing in this book is a trademark: Elmer's®

Library of Congress Cataloging-in-Publication Data
Doudna, Kelly, 1963-
 Super simple twig projects : fun and easy crafts inspired by nature / Kelly Doudna, consulting editor, Diane Craig, M.A./reading specialist.
    pages cm. -- (Super simple nature crafts)
 Audience: Age 5-10.
 ISBN 978-1-62403-083-3
1. Nature craft--Juvenile literature. 2. Twigs--Juvenile literature. I. Title.
 TT157.D683 2014
 745.59--dc23
                        2013022905

Super SandCastle™ books are created by a team of professional educators, reading specialists, and content developers around five essential components—phonemic awareness, phonics, vocabulary, text comprehension, and fluency—to assist young readers as they develop reading skills and strategies and increase their general knowledge. All books are written, reviewed, and leveled for guided reading, early reading intervention, and Accelerated Reader® programs for use in shared, guided, and independent reading and writing activities to support a balanced approach to literacy instruction.

to adult Helpers

The craft projects in this series are fun and simple. There are just a few things to remember to keep kids safe. Some projects require the use of sharp or hot objects. Also, kids may be using messy materials such as glue or paint. Make sure they protect their clothes and work surfaces. Review the projects before starting, and be ready to assist when necessary.

Key Symbols

In this book, you will see some warning symbols. Here is what they mean.

HOT!
You will be working with something hot. Get help!

SHARP!
You will be working with a sharp object. Get help!

contents

terrific twigs

We love to throw sticks for our dogs. We use sticks and twigs to start campfires. But did you know you can get crafty with sticks and twigs? Go on a nature walk. Gather a bunch of sticks and twigs. Then it's time to go inside and get creative! Try the fun and simple projects in this book. You'll find out how **terrific** twigs can be!

about twigs

The parts of a tree that are above ground are the trunk and the crown. The roots are below ground.

The crown is made up of branches and leaves. Twigs are very small branches.

If a twig has a lot of bumps, use nippers to cut them off. Use garden cutters to cut through thicker twigs.

A log cabin is the **ultimate** twig project! But it's made with big tree trunks instead of tiny twigs. A log cabin is made a lot like the Twig Basket in this book (see page 28).

(see page 28).

PRO tiP
Only use twigs and sticks that you find on the ground. Get **permission** before cutting something off a tree or bush.

fun fact
A tree has as many roots as it has branches!

WHat you'll need

Here are many of the things you will need to do the projects in this book. You can find some of them around the house or yard. You can get others at a craft store or hardware store.

twigs

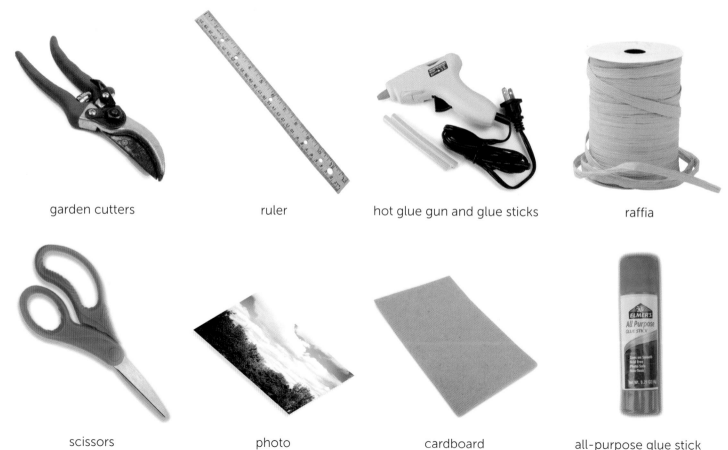

garden cutters

ruler

hot glue gun and glue sticks

raffia

scissors

photo

cardboard

all-purpose glue stick

empty, clean glass jar

ribbon

twine

craft foam

stickers

trailing plant

colored string

beads

feathers

Picture frame

Picture a perfect frame for your photo.

WHAT YOU'LL NEED

straight twigs

garden cutters

ruler

hot glue gun and glue sticks

7 x 9-inch (18 x 23 cm) piece of cardboard

raffia

scissors

5 x 7-inch (12.7 x 18 cm) photo

all-purpose glue stick

1 Use garden cutters to trim the twigs. Cut twelve 9-inch (23 cm) twigs. Cut twelve 11-inch (28 cm) twigs.

2 Lay six of the 9-inch (23 cm) twigs side by side. Glue them together with hot glue. Repeat with the other 9-inch (23 cm) twigs. Glue six 11-inch (28 cm) twigs together the same way. Repeat with the other 11-inch (28 cm) twigs. Let the glue dry.

3 Lay the two 11-inch (28 cm) groups along the long edges of the cardboard. Don't use glue yet. Use the cardboard as a guide for spacing.

continued on the next page

 **pro tip**

Thses twigs were very thin. Use fewer than six per side if your twigs are thicker. The groups should be about 2 inches (5 cm) wide.

4 Put hot glue on the long twigs. Put it about 2 inches (5 cm) from the ends.

5 Lay the groups of short twigs across the long twigs. Press them into the glue. This makes a twig rectangle. Let the glue dry.

6 Wrap raffia around each corner of the twig frame. Make an x pattern. Tie the ends of the raffia together behind the frame.

 get fancy

After step 5, paint the frame with acrylic paint. Use a color that matches your room or the **photo**. Let the paint dry. Then continue with step 6.

7 Use the glue stick to cover the back of the **photo** with glue. Press the photo onto the cardboard. Center it on the cardboard.

8 Put hot glue on each corner of the cardboard. Press the twig frame onto the cardboard. Let the glue dry.

9 Tie each end of a long piece of raffia to the raffia on the top of the frame. This makes a hanger for the frame.

vase

Flowers will look fabulous in this terrific twig vase.

1 Measure the jar. Cut twigs that are at least 1 inch (2.5 cm) longer than the jar is tall. Cut enough twigs to go all the way around the jar.

2 Use hot glue to glue the twigs to the jar. One end of each twig should be even with the bottom of the jar.

3 Tie a ribbon around the vase.

 Pro tip

This is a good project for twigs that aren't quite straight. If you end up with gaps, fill them in with short twigs.

DESKtOP SHElf

Dress up your desk with this pleasing platform.

WHAT YOU'LL NEED

straight twigs

garden cutters

ruler

twine

scissors

hot glue gun and glue sticks

1 Cut twelve 8-inch (20.3 cm) twigs.

2 Divide the twigs into four groups of three.

3 Tie each group of twigs together with twine.

4 Hold two twig **bundles** in an x shape. Wrap twine around the bundles where they meet. Repeat with the other two bundles. These are the legs for the **shelf**.

continued on the next page

5 Cut two 6-inch (15.2 cm) twigs.

6 Cut several 12-inch (30.5 cm) twigs.

7 Lay the long twigs side by side. They should take up 5 inches (15.2 cm).

8 Hot glue one end of each long twig to one of the short twigs. Glue the other end of each long twig to the second short twig. This is the **shelf**.

9 Turn the **shelf** over. Put a dot of hot glue on either side of the shelf near the short twig.

10 Set the shelf on one x-shaped piece. The x should touch the shelf where the glue is. Hold the shelf level while the glue sets.

11 Follow steps 9 and 10 with the other end of the shelf and the other x-shaped piece.

12 Let the glue dry.

 Pro tip

Use longer or shorter twigs to make this shelf any size. Just remember that it isn't strong enough to hold heavy things.

raft

Have floating fun with this rustic raft.

WHAT YOU'LL NEED

twigs

garden cutters

ruler

hot glue gun and glue sticks

thin twine

craft foam

scissors

stickers

1. Cut two 4-inch (10 cm) twigs.

2. Cut some 6-inch (15 cm) twigs. Cut enough twigs to take up 3 inches (7.6 cm) when laid side by side.

3. Lay the shorter twigs down about 5 inches (12.7 cm) apart.

4. Put a dot of glue on one end of each shorter twig.

continued on the next page

 **fun fact**

Wood has a lot of air in it. That's why it floats on water.

5 Press a long twig into the glue. The ends should stick out past the short twigs a little bit.

6 Continue hot gluing long twigs over the short twigs until the short twigs are covered.

7 Let the glue dry. This is the **raft**.

8 Wind twine over and under the ends of the long twigs. Go back and forth. Tie the twine in a knot on the bottom of the raft. Use a small dot of hot glue to hold the knot. Trim the ends of the twine. Repeat on the other end of the raft.

9 Cut a 7-inch (18 cm) twig. This is the mast.

10 Cut a right triangle out of craft foam. The vertical side should be 4 inches (10 cm) long. The **horizontal** side should be a little shorter. This is the sail.

11 Hot glue the twig to the 4-inch (10 cm) side of the triangle. Let the glue dry.

12 Decorate the sail with stickers.

13 Put some hot glue at one end of the **raft**. Put it on a twig near the middle. Set the bottom of the mast in the glue. Hold it up until the glue sets.

 fun tip

Float your raft in the bathtub. Or take your raft to a beach or a swimming pool. Have races with your friends.

 safety tip

Remember to put safety first. An adult should be with you if you are near water.

flower pot trellis

Train your trailing plant to try this trellis.

WHAT YOU'LL NEED

twigs

garden cutters

ruler

trailing plant (such as ivy or pathos) planted in a 6-inch (15 cm) pot

twine

scissors

1. Cut three twigs that are 18 inches (46 cm) long. Stick them into the dirt. Space them evenly around the pot.

2. Cut three twigs that are 7 inches (18 cm) long. Cut three more twigs that are 9 inches (23 cm) long.

3. Hold a 7-inch (18 cm) twig 4 inches (10 cm) above the pot. Hold it across two of the upright twigs.

4. Use twine to tie the end of the short twig to the upright twig. Repeat with the other end of the short twig.

5. Tie the other two 7-inch (18 cm) twigs to other two sides. You should end up with a triangle around the upright twigs.

6. Tie the three 9-inch (23 cm) twigs horizontally to the upright twigs. They should be about 8 inches (20 cm) above the pot.

7. Set your pot by a window. Wind the plant around the twig trellis as it grows.

DREAM CATCHER

You'll sleep sweetly with a dream catcher on your wall.

WHAT YOU'LL NEED

six 5-inch (12.7 cm) twigs

garden cutters

hot glue gun and glue sticks

colored string

scissors

12 beads

ruler

3 feathers

Making the Web

1 Hot glue the twig ends together to make a **hexagon**. Let the glue dry.

2 Wrap and then tie string around each corner of the hexagon. This will make the dream catcher stronger. Trim the ends of the string.

3 ROUND 1. Tie the end of a long piece of string around the middle of one of the twigs.

4 Tie the string around the middle of the next twig. Continue until all the twigs have a knot. Put a bead on the string before tying one of the knots.

continued on the next page

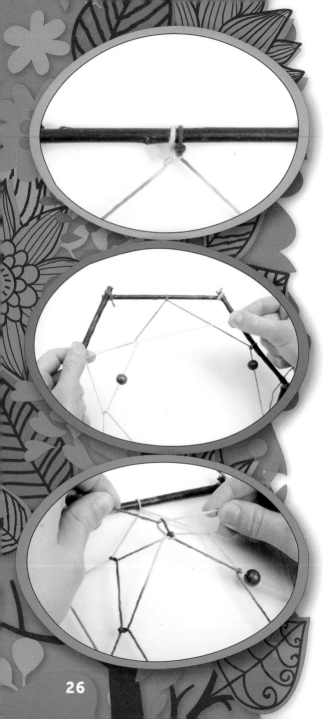

5 Tie the string to the twig next to the first knot. Trim the string close to the final knot.

6 **ROUND 2.** Cut a second long piece of string. Tie the second string to each straight section of the first string. Follow the same steps as you did for tying the first string to the twigs. Put a bead on the string before tying one of the knots.

7 Tie the string next to the first knot. Cut the string close to the final knot.

8 **ROUND 3.** Cut a third long piece of string. Tie the third string to each straight section of the second string. Follow the same steps as you did for tying the second string to the first string. Put a bead on the string before tying one of the knots.

9 Tie the string next to the first knot. Trim the string close to the final knot.

Finishing

1 Cut three 6-inch (15.2 cm) pieces of string. Tie one end of each string to a single feather.

2 Put three beads on each string.

3 Tie the three feather strings to one twig. This is the bottom of the dream catcher.

4 Tie a 16-inch (40.6 cm) string to the top of the dream catcher to make a hanger.

5 Trim any long ends of string.

 **fun fact**

Dream catchers come from the First Nations **culture**. Good dreams find their way through the web. They flow from the feathers to the dreamer. Bad dreams get caught in the web. They don't find their way to the dreamer.

Basket

Take time to tidy up using this basic basket.

twigs
ruler
garden cutters
hot glue gun
and glue sticks
ribbon
scissors

1. Cut six 10-inch (25.4 cm) twigs. Lay them side by side about ½ inch (1.3 cm) apart.

2. Measure how much space the twigs take up. Add 2 inches (5 cm) to that number. That's your final **measurement**.

3. Cut two twigs as long as your final measurement from step 2. Lay one across each end of the six twigs.

4. Put hot glue where the top twigs touch the bottom twigs. Press the twigs into the glue. Let the glue dry.

5. Turn the piece over. The long twigs should be on top. This is the bottom of the basket.

6. Cut two twigs 1 inch (2.5 cm) longer than your step 2 measurement. Lay one across each short side of the basket. Glue them in place.

continued on the next page

7 Cut two 11-inch (28 cm) twigs. Lay one across each long side. Glue them in place.

8 Continue adding twigs to alternating sides of the basket. Add 1 inch (2.5 cm) to the length of the twigs each time. Add twigs until the basket is about 6 inches (15.2 cm) deep. Let the glue dry.

9 Weave ribbon back and forth between the bottom twigs. Glue the ribbon ends to the twigs.

10 Wind ribbon around each of the four top twigs. Glue the ends to the twigs.

 Pro tip

This is a good project for twigs that aren't quite straight.

conclusion

Aren't twigs great? You have let the beauty of nature come through with these wonderful twig crafts. If you had fun, don't stop here. How else can you use twigs?

And check out the other books in the Super Simple Nature Crafts series. You'll find projects that use ice, leaves, pinecones, pressed flowers, and seashells. The ideas are endless!

glossary

bundle – a group of things tied together.

culture – the ideas, traditions, art, and behaviors of a group of people.

hexagon – a shape that has six equal sides and six equal angles.

horizontal – in the same direction as the ground, or side-to-side.

measurement – a piece of information found by measuring.

permission – when a person in charge says it's okay to do something.

photo – a picture made using a camera.

raft – a flat boat or mat used to float on water.

shelf – a thin, flat surface used to store things.

terrific – great or wonderful.

ultimate – being the best or greatest.